DEATH SINGS IN THE SHADOWS

Bryan Stubbles

BROADWAY PLAY PUBLISHING INC
New York
www.broadwayplaypublishing.com
info@broadwayplaypublishing.com

Cover photo of Victoria Sethunya by Bryan Stubbles. Cover graphic design by Mark Hatting.

First edition: September 2017
I S B N: 978-0-88145-735-3

Book design: Marie Donovan
Page make-up: Adobe InDesign
Typeface: Palatino

CHARACTERS

WESLEY "BRIGHAM" THURMAN, (20s-30s): *Utah-born African-American medic. In over his head. An outsider. Wears a U S Army uniform at beginning. Talks like anyone else from Utah.*

PRINCESS, (20s-40s): *Native Liberian jazz singer. She wears a Liberian lappa. She speaks Liberian Pidgin English, not her native language.*

ALBERTINE, (20s-40s): *Americo-Liberian good-time gal. Wears a slinky dress and heels. Speaks Liberian Settler English.*

CAPTAIN MICHAUX, (20s-60s): *Americo-Liberian Frontier Force officer and Monrovia policeman. Imperious. Arrogant. Tan uniform. Laughs too much. Speaks Liberian Settler English.*

SERGEANT ROSS, (40s-50s): *African-American sergeant. W W I vet. THURMAN's confidant. From the Deep South. Seen it all.*

ESTHER, (20s-40s): *African-American missionary from Detroit. Wears a beautiful American dress. Talks like she graduated from Spelman.*

HEART MAN, (40s+): *Native Liberian shaman. Grebo. Good guy. Speaks Liberian Pidgin English.*

EDWIN BARCLAY, (61): *Americo-Liberian president. Uncle was also president. Beautiful suit. Distinguished air about him. Speaks Liberian Settler English.*

SETTING

Monrovia, Liberia, 1943. World War II. Liberia is a cauldron. Five percent of Liberians, called Americo-Liberians (descendants of 19th Century African-American colonists) repress the other 95% (native Liberians).They live well. The other 95% don't. American soldiers (mostly black) are in the country protecting the Firestone rubber plantation and building an airfield.

Set: Minimalist stage (ie: a table for a bar).

Music: All songs in the public domain.

Dialect: dialect and accent play a huge role in this play. I trust the actors 100%. Brief notes covering the forms of Liberian English in the play.

Liberian Pidgin English: Nobody's first language, but a pidgin spoken by HEART MAN *and* PRINCESS. *The dialect clips many of the final syllables with a nasal stress. No "th" sound.*

Liberian Settler English: The language of the descendants of American settlers, like a mix between African-American Vernacular English and Jamaican Patois. Presidents Charles Taylor and Ellen Johnson-Sirleaf speak like this. The language of ALBERTINE, MICHAUX *and* BARCLAY.

Liberian glossary from the play:
Cohloh/colored boy = old word for an African American
Kwi = civilized
Fish = vagina (slang)
Come-here = a recent arrival in Liberia (archaic)
A L, Merico, Congo = Americo-Liberian. In addition to American settlers, "liberated" Africans from slave ships were deposited in Monrovia by the U S and British navies. Many came from the Congo.
Finish = completely. Finish drunk: blotto
Watapolee = promiscuous woman
Bachelor girl = single woman, pejorative. Many Liberians add an "-o" to words for emphasis.

Special thanks to Comfort Tana Whitfield for serving as technical advisor.

ACT ONE

Scene 1: The "Lone Star" —a jazz bar in Monrovia, Liberia, 1943

Scene 2: Makeshift morgue

Scene 3: Esther's living room

Scene 4: Jail cell

Scene 5: Hospital room

Scene 6: The "Lone Star"

ACT TWO

Scene 1: The "Lone Star"

Scene 2: Monrovia alleyway

Scene 3: Jail cell

Scene 4: Hospital room

Scene 5: Esther's living room

Scene 6: Esther's living room

ACT ONE

Scene 1

(Lights up:)

(A simple jazz club. "The Lone Star." The Liberian flag hangs length-wise in the background [the star is on the upper-right, stripes face down].)

(Lights on:)

(PRINCESS. A period microphone in front of her)

(She sings "Saint James' Infirmary" with musical accompaniment from off-stage.)

PRINCESS: *(Singing, as sultry as they come)*
Folks, I'm goin' down to St. James Infirmary,
See my baby there;
She's stretched out on a long, white table,
So sweet, so cold, so fair.
Let it go, let it go, God bless her,
Wherever she may be,
She can search this whole wide world over,
But she'll never find another sweet man like me.
When I die, bury me in my straight-leg britches,
Put on a box-back coat and a Stetson hat,
Put a twenty-dollar gold piece on my watch chain,
So you can let all the boys know I died standing pat.
An' give me six crap shooting pall bearers,
Let a chorus girl sing me a song.
Put a red hot jazz band at the top of my head

So we can raise Hallelujah as we go along.
Folks, now that you have heard my story,
Say, boy, hand me another shot of that booze;
If anyone should ask you,
You just tell 'em I've got those Saint James Infirmary
blues.

(Applause from O S)

PRINCESS: Thank you plenty. Ten minute break!

(Ironically, her song was in perfect American English. Exit PRINCESS. *Lights down.)*

(Lights on:)

(An African-American man, WESLEY "BRIGHAM"
THURMAN, *30, sits on a bar stool in front of a table. Wears a U S Army uniform and reads a newspaper.)*

*(*ALBERTINE *on a stool next to him. A drink in front of her.)*

ALBERTINE: You like her?

*(*BRIGHAM *lost in thought.* ALBERTINE *playfully pokes him.)*

BRIGHAM: Oh, hey. Didn't see ya.

ALBERTINE: I ax, do you like her?

BRIGHAM: Easy on the ears.

ALBERTINE: And eyes.

*(*BRIGHAM *laughs.)*

*(*ALBERTINE *takes his wrist, as if admiring the skin tone on the back of his hand. She notices his watch.)*

ALBERTINE: It's late.

BRIGHAM: Do you have an appointment?

ALBERTINE: Not yet, Yankee. *(Sips drink)* You talk kwi.

BRIGHAM: Excuse me?

ALBERTINE: Kwi. Means "civilized".

BRIGHAM: Who is civilized and who is savage?

ALBERTINE: You don' talk like no cohloh boy.

(BRIGHAM *laughs*.)

BRIGHAM: Neither do you.

ALBERTINE: What you mean? I'm the queen o' kwi. I'm from North Carolina.

(BRIGHAM *laughs at* ALBERTINE*'s lie*.)

BRIGHAM: North Carolina, huh? What town?

ALBERTINE: Tennessee.

BRIGHAM: You're from right here in Monrovia. *(He looks* ALBERTINE *up and down.)* Water Street? Nellie Hagar's place?

(ALBERTINE *slaps* BRIGHAM.)

ALBERTINE: I don't work for no Nellie Hagar. I'm a respectable Americo-Liberian woman. I'm civilized.

BRIGHAM: Maybe your great-great-granddaddy came from Winston-Salem. But you didn't.

ALBERTINE: Winston-Salem! Full of witches.

BRIGHAM: Let me tell you—

(ALBERTINE *stands up*.)

ALBERTINE: Let me tell you. American history is Liberian history. We got more witches here than America dreamed of. *(Takes a drink)* Baby, you a missionary?

(BRIGHAM *gestures to his uniform*.)

BRIGHAM: Killing Nazis is my mission.

(ALBERTINE *laughs*.)

ALBERTINE: Nazis in Liberia? They lost!

BRIGHAM: We defend the Firestone plantation from Nazis.

ALBERTINE: You defend the plantation? *(She giggles. She points to insignia on his uniform.)* Doctor.

BRIGHAM: I render medical aid to those sick and injured.

ALBERTINE: Now I know why Liberians lie so much. Cohloh boy lie too!

(ALBERTINE behind BRIGHAM. Reaches her arm around his neck. Leans on him)

BRIGHAM: I treat V D cases.

(ALBERTINE lets go of BRIGHAM.)

(BRIGHAM turns and looks at ALBERTINE.)

ALBERTINE: We could make a racket. You a man of medicine. That's why I thought you was a missionary.

BRIGHAM: A missionary in a bar?

ALBERTINE: You where the sinners at.

(No answer)

ALBERTINE: Missionary is the greatest sinner of all.

(ALBERTINE laughs. She rubs her leg against his. She looks squarely at a bulge in BRIGHAM's pocket.)

ALBERTINE: Thought you had to leave the pistol on base.

BRIGHAM: Actually—I'm a conscientious objector.

ALBERTINE: Then what that in your pocket-o?

BRIGHAM: I don't carry a gun.

ALBERTINE: A soldier with no gun? You stupid.

BRIGHAM: I cannot kill a man.

(ALBERTINE grabs for BRIGHAM's pocket.)

ALBERTINE: What?

BRIGHAM: *(Feigns ignorance)* Naw. This is for my sweetheart.

(ALBERTINE *breaks off the leg action.*)

ALBERTINE: If she so sweet, why you alone?

(BRIGHAM *looks at his watch.*)

BRIGHAM: She's on her way.

ALBERTINE: Maybe she get another meeting tonight.

BRIGHAM: Betty's an Army nurse. Punctuality comes with the job.

ALBERTINE: She American?

BRIGHAM: One-hundred percent.

ALBERTINE: Stand up a doctor? She don't treat you right-o. You need good Liberian woman for take good care of you.

(ALBERTINE *grabs the bulge. Surprise! She pulls away like kryptonite.* BRIGHAM *laughs.*)

(BRIGHAM *takes out a hard little box.* ALBERTINE *looks disappointed.*)

(BRIGHAM *opens it. A ring*)

ALBERTINE: You gonna propose? *(She sits down.)* Mister Big-shot. The Big Man of Monrovia. How you gonna do it?

BRIGHAM: I'm working on that.

ALBERTINE: I figured you knew your way around a woman, Medicine Man.

BRIGHAM: Any ideas?

(ALBERTINE *looks around the club.*)

ALBERTINE: Not in this den of iniquity. Take her to the beach.

(ALBERTINE *pulls* BRIGHAM *up. They stand.*)

(*She grabs his arm.*)

ALBERTINE: How you lead a woman, Yankee?

BRIGHAM: Can I finish my paper?

ALBERTINE: No! You wasn't even reading it. Treat me like a lady.

BRIGHAM: That's a stretch.

(ALBERTINE *raises her hand to smack* BRIGHAM—*he catches it.*)

BRIGHAM: Sorry. We sit. The beach. On a towel maybe.

ALBERTINE: *(Points to audience)* Look. The Atlantic.

BRIGHAM: I crossed that bucket of water in a hull. You'd think a medic couldn't get seasick. You'd be wrong.

ALBERTINE: My people got the round-trip ticket. *(Gestures as she talks)* First they go one way. Sold to America. A few lifespan later, America send them back. Here. My home.

(ALBERTINE *hangs on* BRIGHAM. *Points)*

ALBERTINE: The sunset. Beautiful. *(She points to the floor.)* Blanket here.

(ALBERTINE *and* BRIGHAM *sit on the floor.)*

ALBERTINE: We friends?

BRIGHAM: I don't know your name.

ALBERTINE: Relax, Yankee! Albertine.

(ALBERTINE *kisses* BRIGHAM. *He backs off.)*

ALBERTINE: Propose marriage.

(BRIGHAM *pulls the ring out.)*

BRIGHAM: Practice.

ALBERTINE: Practice.

BRIGHAM: Will you marry me?

ALBERTINE: You know the answer.

(ALBERTINE *sticks her hand out for the ring.* BRIGHAM *puts it on.*)

ALBERTINE: Any woman would be happy with you. Even a woman you don't know, she could love you.

(BRIGHAM *quickly takes it back.*)

ALBERTINE looks at his watch.)

ALBERTINE: It's late! *(She stands up.)* Sorry, baby. *(She runs and exits.)*

(BRIGHAM *looks around. He shrugs. Off-stage, a blood-freezing scream.*)

(BRIGHAM *stands up, runs off-stage and exits.*)

(Lights down:)

Scene 2

(Lights up:)

(A makeshift examination room. A table with Betty's body, covered by a blood-soaked shroud.)

(BRIGHAM *with two men, in different uniforms:* CAPTAIN MICHAUX, *and* SERGEANT ROSS.)

MICHAUX: The Government of the Republic of Liberia would be very interested in conducting the investigation ourselves.

ROSS: Put her on ice.

MICHAUX: But the republic stands temporarily short on funds, due to—due to the exigencies accompanying the relocation of American troops here. Indefinitely. We must sacrifice for the war.

ROSS: *(To* BRIGHAM*)* Who that actor? Got a monocle on his face? Kraut-eatin' Hun-type guy.

BRIGHAM: Erich von Stroheim?

ROSS: His Liberian cousin.

MICHAUX: I am not Von Stroheim. I am Major Alfred Russell Xavier Michaux, Monrovia special police and Captain of the Liberian Frontier Force. My father was superintendent of Mesurado County. My grandfather a senator and my great-grandmother was born free in Ohio.

ROSS: Is you a captain or a major?

MICHAUX: I'm both. I'm Michaux.

ROSS: You got a frog name, Michaux. I met many frogs in the first war.

(MICHAUX *pulls his pistol.*)

MICHAUX: I am not a frog!

ROSS: Toad.

BRIGHAM: Sergeant Ross—

MICHAUX: Yes, Sergeant. Listen to your friend. Do not insult an officer of the Monrovia Police Department and the Liberian Frontier Force! You are only a sergeant. I shall have you reprimanded.

ROSS: Right after you learn how to spell "reprimand".

MICHAUX: I kill you!

(BRIGHAM *disarms* MICHAUX *quickly.*)

BRIGHAM: Betty is dead. And you play with your goddamned pea shooters.

MICHAUX: Apologies. The heat of the moment you know. French blood. *(Bows)*

ROSS: *(To* BRIGHAM*)* You shaken. But we need an autopsy.

(BRIGHAM *hands the pistol back to* MICHAUX.)

ROSS: You ain't in Utah no more. If I could do an autopsy I would. You our only medical staff fit for duty now.

BRIGHAM: Where's Dr Willis?

ROSS: Failed short-arm inspection.

BRIGHAM: Typical white man in Africa. No surprise there.

MICHAUX: Leopard men!

(ROSS and BRIGHAM look at MICHAUX like he's mad.)

BRIGHAM: I'm certain a person did this.

MICHAUX: A leopard man! Is she lacking her uterus? Many aboriginals take uteruses for their witching. Heart. Uterus. Eyes.

(MICHAUX walks to the table like he's gonna rip the shroud off. ROSS and BRIGHAM stop him.)

MICHAUX: You colored boys hiding something?

ROSS: Her dignity.

BRIGHAM: *(To ROSS)* It's his job, Sergeant Ross.

(ROSS pulls the sheet back quickly. BRIGHAM doesn't look.)

(BRIGHAM and MICHAUX block the audience's view. When MICHAUX sees her face, he screams and jumps back. ROSS puts the sheet back.)

(The audience sees nothing but the men's reactions.)

MICHAUX: An aborigine did this. They always cuttin' the organs for rituals.

ROSS: Her eyes?

MICHAUX: Better to see one's enemies. Aborigines.

ROSS: Don't lay this on your second-class citizens.

MICHAUX: They are not even citizens.

ROSS: Those missing eyes cloud up your vision.

MICHAUX: Your ancestors were slaves. What do you know?

ROSS: So were yours.

MICHAUX: You Americans think you can come here and push Liberia around? Please don't imagine this is city mouse, country mouse—rich cousin, poor cousin. We are the rich cousin here. We have our own country. We've had sixteen presidents, all Negros. In your country you can't even vote.

BRIGHAM: I can't do an autopsy. I'm just a physician's assistant in civilian life.

ROSS: You loved her.

ROSS: Then the autopsy needs to happen.

BRIGHAM: I can't.

ROSS: Whatever, Utah.

BRIGHAM: Stop with the Utah cracks. I outrank you anyways. I don't carry on about your hometown.

ROSS: The boys in our outfit just can't get over a Negro from the Mormon State. Brigham.

BRIGHAM: I'm not even Mormon. My name's Wesley. It's those slick sleeve yahoos who gave me the name Brigham.

ROSS: What's in a name?

BRIGHAM: My girlfriend is dead and we carry on about this?

ROSS: Tryna ease the tension. Nobody want to see you in that bad place, Brig. I'll look at her for you. It sure as Hell would beat 1918. *(To* MICHAUX*)* Have you seen mustard gas? Nerve gas? Chlorine? Bodies bayoneted like a pin cushion—

MICHAUX: Bodies?

ROSS: All along the trench.

MICHAUX: You have the experience. You look at the Leopard Men's business. Then report to me.

(ROSS *takes* BRIGHAM *away from* MICHAUX.)

ROSS: Don't let this fool take charge.

BRIGHAM: That's not happening.

ROSS: I know you Brigham. You too nice.

BRIGHAM: I've got this.

MICHAUX: Secrets?

(ROSS *raises his voice.*)

ROSS: Did she tell her kinfolk about ya?

BRIGHAM: She did.

ROSS: Figure they need the truth? You need the truth?

BRIGHAM: Of course.

ROSS: If I was a doctor, I'd fix the whole thing myself. I ain't. You is. You save lives. This one is gone, but you can help justice. *(Pause)* These new soldiers complain about building airstrips, ports, guarding Firestone and listening to tom-toms at night. And not fighting. I fought the Hun in One. Death and violence never escape my dreams, son. *(Looks at the body and* MICHAUX*)* You got a murder to figure out. Don't let fear or stupidity haunt you. *(He walks toward off-stage.)*

BRIGHAM: You're not gonna assist me?

ROSS: *(Big smile, to* MICHAUX*)*) As they said in the Saint-Mihiel Offensive, adieu!

BRIGHAM: Sergeant!

(ROSS *freezes.)*

ROSS: Lieutenant.

BRIGHAM: You just got paid?

ROSS: Yes, sir.

BRIGHAM: Don't spend it all in one place.

(ROSS *exits*.)

MICHAUX: What a hilarious backwards colored boy!

BRIGHAM: Best N C O I know.

MICHAUX: In his forties and already an N C O. If he were Liberian, he could be president by now.

BRIGHAM: He's smarter than that.

MICHAUX: What?

BRIGHAM: Nothing. Let's get to work.

MICHAUX: Perhaps you could be president—

BRIGHAM: I need a camera, a pencil and a notebook.

MICHAUX: We have a Brownie in the office.

(BRIGHAM *looks at* MICHAUX.)

MICHAUX: I am an officer of Liberian Frontier Force!

BRIGHAM: The frontier's two hundred miles from here.

(MICHAUX *yells to off-stage. More pidginized English.*)

MICHAUX: Private Dweh! Come! Bring Brownie, paper, pencil! Now! (*No response*) Dweh! Country boy lazy too much! (*He looks O S.*)

BRIGHAM: (*To himself*) Lazy too much.

(MICHAUX *turns and looks at* BRIGHAM. *Back to "kwi" Americo-Liberian English.*)

MICHAUX: An officer of the Liberian Frontier Force and the Monrovia Police fetches for nobody. (*Exits. From off-stage*) Lazy too much!

(BRIGHAM *walks behind the body and faces the body and audience. He bows his head in silent prayer. Hold for a few precious moments.*)

(*The Kodak Brownie flies onto the stage from O S.*)

BRIGHAM: Michaux? Dweh! Where is your captain? *(He sighs. He tries Liberian Pidgin English.)* Where you captain? I beat you! *(He laughs to himself. Picks up the camera. Still in dialect.)* Thank you plenty! *(He lifts the shroud just as—)*

(Lights down:)

(Several seconds)

(Lights up:)

(The same place. Several hours later. BRIGHAM sits on the apron, exhausted. Blood on him)

(Papers on the floor next to him. O S tom-tom music plays throughout.)

(MICHAUX and ROSS stand. ROSS coughs.)

BRIGHAM: Oh. *(He stands up. He hands papers to each.)* Mimeographed my report.

ROSS: *(Reading)* Toe. Finger. Voice box. Heart. Breast. Uterus. Tongue. Eyes. And that?

BRIGHAM: All gone.

MICHAUX: Leopard Men!

BRIGHAM: Humans. Not cats.

MICHAUX: You don't know their power.

BRIGHAM: Are they stronger than you?

MICHAUX: Oh, no. Never.

BRIGHAM: Then don't worry.

MICHAUX: I'm just warning you—of their blackhearted desire.

ROSS: Blackhearted?

(ROSS and BRIGHAM look at each other.)

ROSS: *(To MICHAUX)* Captain, these men you blamin', they bleed same as us.

MICHAUX: You are new to Liberia. You are "come-here." You don't know. My people—We gave them everything they have now. Yet they persist in their wicked, wicked ways. *(Smile)* Besides, I never answer to white men like American coloh boy do.

(ROSS *and* BRIGHAM *let the insult slide.)*

ROSS: Tell Brig 'bout these Leopard Men.

MICHAUX: Witching. Someone make witch.

BRIGHAM: How does one "make witch"?

MICHAUX: One witch enter a man o' woman. That witch then infect, control that man o' woman. Makes terrible things happen.

BRIGHAM: A witch isn't a leopard.

MICHAUX: A Leopard Society exists. Its people are owned by the witch. I think you say spirit. They kill people in the bush. Sometimes in Monrovia. On Water Street.

BRIGHAM: Why kill an American?

MICHAUX: Easier to kill than a Liberian.

ROSS: How?

MICHAUX: I don't mean to insult you, but Americans are weak. You've been away too long. You lack the robust vigor of a Liberian. And when you come, like all these soldiers…you get every disease imaginable. And new ones, too. You should call them "Yankee Flu"— "Yankee Typhoid" and "Yankee Fever".

ROSS: The Leopard Men? Is this some type of voodoo? Hoodoo?

MICHAUX: This, my friends, is African Science. A heart may give courage or love. Eyes can give clarity of purpose. A uterus can give reproductive powers.

Americans don't understand African Science. Cooking or eating—

ROSS: What is the cause of death?

BRIGHAM: It's on Michaux' paper. Unknown, but definitely homicide.

MICHAUX: Are you a pathologist?

BRIGHAM: I was a medical student at the University of Utah who got sucked up in a world war and shipped off to Liberia where I fell in love with an Army nurse who is now dead and missing her organs and has a smile carved on her face. I know it's murder.

MICHAUX: That's not in the paper.

(BRIGHAM *grabs the paper and points for* MICHAUX.)

MICHAUX: Yes, I see.

BRIGHAM: I will find her killer.

MICHAUX: At your service.

BRIGHAM: Round up these Leopard Men you're so fond of.

MICHAUX: I knew you would see the way—of African Science.

ROSS: Make sure they don't change their spots.

MICHAUX: Don't tell me how to do my job. I want a proper medical man and they give me you. A Utah Negro. Mormon.

BRIGHAM: I'll do anything to find her killer.

MICHAUX: Have faith in the great Liberian—

ROSS: Oh, we do.

BRIGHAM: Check back tomorrow, Captain.

(MICHAUX *weakly salutes and exits.*)

BRIGHAM: Reckon he killed her?

ROSS: He's too stupid.

BRIGHAM: Hey, Sergeant. Do you know the chaplain?

ROSS: Friar Tuck? He's using up my dose of penicillin presently. May not be the most inspiring man of God in this land.

BRIGHAM: The chaplain? Really?

ROSS: But I know a missionary gal.

BRIGHAM: A gal?

ROSS: A coal scuttle blonde. You got coal scuttle blondes in Salt Lake? She a missionary here for the Liberians but she from the States.

(Drums stop O S.)

(Lights down:)

Scene 3

(Lights up:)

(ESTHER's house)

(ESTHER stands in front of BRIGHAM.)

ESTHER: Take a seat, Lieutenant.

BRIGHAM: Thank you, ma'am.

ESTHER: Southern manners.

BRIGHAM: I'm from—

ESTHER: Utah. Sergeant Ross told me. Thank the good Lord you aren't Mormon.

BRIGHAM: Heck—uh, Hell no. And you? 'Bama?

ESTHER: *(Imitating BRIGHAM)* Heck no. God saw fit for me to be born in Detroit City. Coffee?

BRIGHAM: Sure.

ESTHER: Must be lukewarm by now. Let me heat it up.

BRIGHAM: I take it lukewarm.

ESTHER: Not in the house of Esther you don't. *(She turns the burner on. Sugar? (Pause) In your coffee.*

(BRIGHAM shakes his head "no")

ESTHER: That's not why you're here. *(She sits down in the chair. A thick bible in the chair. She picks it up and holds it close to her.)*

BRIGHAM: Can't make sense of it.

ESTHER: You won't get far second-guessing God.

BRIGHAM: Did God condone this?

ESTHER: Women and men have free will. God sets it up—people follow through. For better or worse.

BRIGHAM: Why? She never hurt nobody.

ESTHER: Whoever did it—they have the heart of a coward.

BRIGHAM: *(Pause)* Did you know her?

ESTHER: I met her. We exchanged pleasantries at an embassy function. She was so beautiful.

BRIGHAM: I remember. The Liberian girls danced the quadrille and the embassy staff got scared when the girls danced the Lindy hop.

ESTHER: The same one.

BRIGHAM: I was there. Don't remember you.

ESTHER: *(Quoting King James Bible John 16:33)* "In the world ye shall have tribulation."

BRIGHAM: He wasn't lyin' about that.

(ESTHER walks back to the coffee and pours a cup for him and a cup for herself. She carries it to BRIGHAM.)

ESTHER: No sugar.

(BRIGHAM sips coffee.)

ESTHER: Too bitter? *(She sits in the chair next to* BRIGHAM. *Quoting Matthew 5:4)* Blessed they that mourn: for they shall be comforted.

BRIGHAM: How can we be sure?

*(*ESTHER *drinks her coffee.)*

ESTHER: The disciples were in mourning after the crucifixion, right?

BRIGHAM: Yeah.

ESTHER: And the savior appeared to them. All were amazed and comforted.

BRIGHAM: I guess so. But this is so different. We're talking a brutal killing. This isn't Palestine two thousand years ago. This is Monrovia. Anno Domini 1943.

ESTHER: We need to pray about this.

*(*BRIGHAM *bows his head.* ESTHER *holds his hand but also puts her arm on him. A little too close for comfort.)*

ESTHER: Lord God, we come to you beseeching peace for Brother Wesley. Peace in his heart, his life, his mind and his soul. We ask that this murdered nurse's family find some peace. She was a sister, a daughter, a grand-daughter, a friend and many things to many people. Help Brother Wesley overcome his grief and see your purpose. There is a reason behind everything. By the Blood of the Lamb I cry out for justice in this matter. *(Quotes Jeremiah 22:3, as she speaks, she gets even closer to him)* Thus saith the Lord; Execute ye judgment and righteousness, and deliver the spoiled out of the hand of the oppressor: and do no wrong, do no violence to the stranger, the fatherless, nor the widow, neither shed innocent blood in this place. These things we ask in Jesus' name.

BRIGHAM: Amen?

ESTHER: Amen. You're warm. Do you have a fever?

BRIGHAM: It's just the heat and the emotion.

ESTHER: I been in the Liberian heat too long.

(BRIGHAM *steps back and sits back down in the chair.*)

ESTHER: What are you afraid of, Brother Wesley?

BRIGHAM: I'm afraid of women here who know my Christian name. (*He stands up.*)

ESTHER: Ross told me.

BRIGHAM: You must have your hands full with him.

ESTHER: God loves even a sinner.

BRIGHAM: God stands on my side in this.

(ESTHER *stands up.*)

ESTHER: You're going back to that bar.

BRIGHAM: You have me all figured out.

ESTHER: But I don't!

(*O S native drums start up.* ESTHER *calms.*)

ESTHER: Please don't go there.

(BRIGHAM *paraphrases Matthew 23:33.*)

BRIGHAM: Those serpents, that generation of vipers, how can they escape the damnation of hell?

ESTHER: They can't.

BRIGHAM: Whatever Satanic fiend did this, he inhabits that den of iniquity. I'll find him.

(ESTHER *walks in front of* BRIGHAM.)

ESTHER: Let me help.

BRIGHAM: Your spiritual guidance helped immensely.

ESTHER: I just read from the Bible and prayed for you.

BRIGHAM: And that's what I needed.

ESTHER: There is spiritual help and then there's practical. Monrovia isn't safe at night.

BRIGHAM: Leopard men?

ESTHER: Leopard Society. Crocodile Society. They are real.

BRIGHAM: I'm not some wild game expert, but I know a crocodile didn't do this.

ESTHER: *(Pause)* Do the police think it was the work of leopard men?

BRIGHAM: I'm not sure the police can even think.

ESTHER: Michaux?

BRIGHAM: You two pals?

ESTHER: Not friends.

BRIGHAM: What's your business with him?

ESTHER takes out a book of matches, a cigarette and lights it. Long drag.

ESTHER: He's around.

BRIGHAM: Around or—

ESTHER: I'm just a lil' ol' Detroit gal all alone.

BRIGHAM: Your fancy house can keep you company.

ESTHER: I do have servants.

BRIGHAM: Where?

ESTHER: They're on errands. You know you can send them on an errand and they might not come back for days. Unpredictably predictable creatures.

BRIGHAM: How does that work?

ESTHER: We are shining light into darkness.

BRIGHAM: Now you do sound like Michaux.

ESTHER: Here. This is part of our calling. Of course the Natives—

BRIGHAM: "Aborigines" as they're called here.

ESTHER: Yes, the tribal people.

BRIGHAM: From the Hinterland.

ESTHER: They know the Americo-Liberians. And they hate them.

BRIGHAM: I like their style.

ESTHER: So some are naturally prone to abhor Christianity simply because the wrong Christians live here.

BRIGHAM: You're A M E, right?

ESTHER: Yeah.

BRIGHAM: And this is the way?

ESTHER: They can see an educated American Negro who loves God and who loves them. By working here, they're exposed to holiness and they can speak better English. Have you heard Liberian English?

BRIGHAM: Let's face it. If but for fortune, we would be a Bassa or Grebo from the Hinterland.

ESTHER: True.

BRIGHAM: Or we would be an Americo-Liberian stuffed shirt. They're almost our cousins.

ESTHER: But God has put us in a position—as American Negroes—to civilize both the heathen in the village as well as upbraid the Americos and their wicked, wicked ways.

BRIGHAM: Did you ever upbraid Michaux?

ESTHER: Persistent bugger, isn't he? *(Pontificating)*

Mister Thurman, heart men and Leopard men and the Crocodile Society are real. They attack, kill, mutilate.

BRIGHAM: Have you seen this?

ESTHER: I read about them in the paper.

BRIGHAM: Call Michaux.

ESTHER: More interested in bribes than justice. Rumor is government officials are behind most ritual murders. Our cousins, remember?

(MICHAUX *enters.*)

ESTHER: Country cousins.

(BRIGHAM *and* ESTHER *turn, startled.*)

BRIGHAM: Do Liberians never knock?

MICHAUX: I never knock when I call on my old friend.

BRIGHAM: No bar fights tonight?

MICHAUX: Not with your G Is on curfew. You do know about curfew, don't you?

BRIGHAM: I've been off-base all day. And where are the telephones in Monrovia?

MICHAUX: I won't tell the base commander you missed curfew. I wouldn't want you to get into trouble.

ESTHER: Michaux—

MICHAUX: That's not why I'm here. I arrested a man in your fiancee's murder. I want you to—observe my technique. (*He grabs* BRIGHAM *by the arm and bows to* ESTHER.) Evening, sister.

ESTHER: Stay safe, Wesley!

(*Exit* MICHAUX *and* BRIGHAM. ESTHER *sits in her chair.*)

(*From near the coffee pot, she takes a small bottle of hard liquor, walks back downstage and sits.*)

(*Takes a drink straight from the bottle.*)

(*Puts the cigarette out on her own leg.*)

(*Lights down:*)

(*Lights up:*)

Scene 4

(A cell)

MICHAUX: *(To* BRIGHAM*)* Fit for horses and witch doctors. *(Swings his riding crop around)* Your fiancee's killer.

*(*MICHAUX *kicks the* HEART MAN*.)*

BRIGHAM: Just because you kick him doesn't make a man guilty.

*(*MICHAUX *then whips* HEART MAN*.)*

BRIGHAM: Stop!

(O S the native drums start up.)

MICHAUX: Ask him who the killer is.

BRIGHAM: *(To* HEART MAN*)* Who?

HEART MAN: I kill her.

BRIGHAM: How?

HEART MAN: Knife. Cut her.

MICHAUX: What for?

HEART MAN: For my medicines.

*(*MICHAUX *kicks* HEART MAN *again.* BRIGHAM *holds* MICHAUX' *arm.)*

BRIGHAM: Let me.

MICHAUX: Take your time, coloh boy.

BRIGHAM: *(To* HEART MAN*)* That all?

HEART MAN: I cut everything. Heart. Fish. Make medicines.

MICHAUX: Best stay away. Savages.

HEART MAN: The AL man beat me-o. He need hep' for elect-o.

*(*BRIGHAM *turns to* MICHAUX*.)*

BRIGHAM: A L man?

MICHAUX: Americo-Liberian. *(To* BRIGHAM*)* Ignore the ignorance of a savage. *(He kicks the* HEART MAN.*)* Say it!

HEART MAN: Congo.

MICHAUX: What am I, boy?

HEART MAN: 'Merico-Liberian.

MICHAUX: *(Points to* BRIGHAM*)* And him?

HEART MAN: Coloh boy. Nigga boy.

MICHAUX: *(To* BRIGHAM*)* Such manners. He doesn't respect you. *(To* HEART MAN*)* Good, good. *(To* BRIGHAM*)* He knows his place.

BRIGHAM: *(To* HEART MAN*)* Why?

*(*BRIGHAM *pulls the* HEART MAN *up.)*

HEART MAN: They need medicine for help election-o.

BRIGHAM: *(To* MICHAUX*)* What's this about Americo-Liberian politicians?

*(*MICHAUX *jumps between* BRIGHAM *and the* HEART MAN.*)*

MICHAUX: He is a lying witch doctor from the Hinterland. A country boy.

*(*BRIGHAM *coughs.)*

HEART MAN: You sick, boss.

BRIGHAM: It's the tropics.

MICHAUX: We shall have a trial immediately. *(To* HEART MAN*)* The noose for you!

HEART MAN: *(To* MICHAUX*)* He sick.

MICHAUX: Some doctor, Brigham.

BRIGHAM: Let me do my job.

MICHAUX: Your job is soldier doctor. Not police, not judge, not jury. We will have a trial. With a noose.

(BRIGHAM *very sick by now. Sicker by the minute*)

MICHAUX: We kill 'im like the rat that he is. *(Pushes* HEART MAN *back to the floor)* And the rat that he ate this morning. *(To* BRIGHAM*)* We're God-fearing people. You and I.

BRIGHAM: We may fear God, but we won't fear killers— *(Cough)* —or disease.

(BRIGHAM *falls to the floor. He struggles to stand. Grabs onto* MICHAUX, *who backs off.* BRIGHAM *falls again. Grabs at his chest)*

BRIGHAM: Get help!

(MICHAUX *exits.* BRIGHAM *sits up.)*

HEART MAN: Just tropics. *(Laughs)*

BRIGHAM: *(Cough)* I am sick. Just not as sick as he thinks. Speak freely now.

HEART MAN: Voting. All these True Whig Party men, they want to be boss man. They all related to each other, but they kill one another. Any power. For them, spiritual boss man is political boss man. Boss over man. Senate. President.

BRIGHAM: Keep talking.

HEART MAN: I medicine man-o. No witch doctor-o. I only do good-o. I come Monrovia for my people-o. Help them. They worry for your people. Kwi.

BRIGHAM: Why worry about us?

HEART MAN: You far from home, kwi man.

BRIGHAM: I can handle myself.

(HEART MAN *laughs.)*

HEART MAN: Handle it. This? Too big for you. Too big for Yankee. Go home.

BRIGHAM: I can't go home. Betty's dead and I need your help. Hurry before Officer Stupid comes back.

HEART MAN: We no need kwi people.

BRIGHAM: Americans aren't as "kwi" as they pretend.

HEART MAN: Guarantee. 'Merico do this. One hundred percent.

BRIGHAM: And what becomes of the organs—body pieces?

HEART MAN: In belly.

BRIGHAM: They eat 'em?

HEART MAN: Cook and eat-o.

(BRIGHAM *coughs violently now.*)

HEART MAN: You really sick-o.

BRIGHAM: Someone ate my fiancée?

(HEART MAN *puts his hand on* BRIGHAM's *forehead.*)

HEART MAN: I can help you-o. I medicine man. I help you find killer.

(*Enter* ROSS *running, followed by* MICHAUX.)

(BRIGHAM *stands.* ROSS *holds him.*)

ROSS: Terrible news. Atrocious. Remember the blood you drained from her body? What was left? It's gone.

MICHAUX: Whoever took the blood must've taken the organs. (*He kicks* HEART MAN.)

BRIGHAM: He was with us.

ROSS: Let's go, Brigham.

(ROSS *carries/drags* BRIGHAM. *They exit.* MICHAUX *circles the* HEART MAN. MICHAUX *brandishes the riding crop.* MICHAUX' *Liberian English gets deeper.*)

MICHAUX: You witch the coloh boy.

HEART MAN: No!

MICHAUX: You hex him good.

HEART MAN: *(Speaking Grebo)* Ondu! *("No.")*

MICHAUX: Don't talk no jungle talk here, boy. *(He beats* HEART MAN *with the crop.)* It is not a question. You hex the American.

HEART MAN: I like the American.

MICHAUX: Stupid aborigine.

*(*MICHAUX *takes out his pistol and points it in the* HEART MAN's *face.)*

MICHAUX: Hex the American, or die.

(Lights down:)

(Lights up:)

Scene 5

*(*BRIGHAM *in bed)*

(O S knock knock)

*(*ESTHER *enters, overdressed.)*

BRIGHAM: Just what the doctor ordered.

ESTHER: Stop hurting yourself like this! You push yourself!

*(*ESTHER *seats herself on the foot of his bed.* BRIGHAM *holds up the Bible and hands it to her.)*

BRIGHAM: Which chapter, which verse, mission lady?

*(*ESTHER *takes the Bible and puts it back down on the bed.)*

ESTHER: That can wait.

BRIGHAM: Some church girl.

ESTHER: You need a nurse…to get better.

BRIGHAM: Did you bring any cigarettes?

ESTHER: No. I only smoke when I'm nervous. What's gotten into you?

BRIGHAM: Malaria.

ESTHER: I take my quinine every day. Medic who don't take his quinine.

BRIGHAM: I had my mind on something else. I was distracted.

ESTHER: What distractions?

BRIGHAM: Hey, how'd you get in here?

ESTHER: The good Lord opens the way to all our desires.

BRIGHAM: The Lord sure has things worked out, doesn't he?

ESTHER: Did she have malaria?

BRIGHAM: No. Whatever killed her came straight from Hell.

ESTHER: I'm so sorry for your loss, really.

BRIGHAM: Everyone's sorry, but nobody does a thing about it.

ESTHER: I'm trying!

BRIGHAM: Why would a politician need Betty dead?

ESTHER: I don't know.

BRIGHAM: Aren't you the expert?

ESTHER: I came here to wish you well and this is the thanks I get? An interrogation?

BRIGHAM: Sorry.

ESTHER: I didn't kill her.

BRIGHAM: Somebody evil did.

ESTHER: Who knows what evil lurks in the hearts of men?

BRIGHAM: That's no Bible. That's the radio series.

ESTHER: On a good day, I can catch a New York broadcast of *The Shadow.*

BRIGHAM: Just like a Fury straight from the bowels of Hades.

ESTHER: For a soldier, you talk like a book.

BRIGHAM: Blame the University of Utah. Pre-med. Where'd you go to school?

ESTHER: Bennett College.

BRIGHAM: Never heard of it.

ESTHER: Like Spelman, but smaller.

BRIGHAM: All women?

ESTHER: Yeah. You should transfer.

(BRIGHAM *laughs.*)

ESTHER: I made you laugh. But you never know what women are capable of.

BRIGHAM: Spinster missionaries in West Africa are capable of anything.

ESTHER: You're stupid.

BRIGHAM: Reckon the killer is a woman?

ESTHER: A Native did it. *(She holds his hand.)* You know, Brigham, this could be your blessing from God.

BRIGHAM: Are you crazy? My fiancee is dead. I'm half dead. The killer is out there. The police are corrupt and—

ESTHER: People need saving. Like Christ. But you do the saving. From sin. *(She lays her head on his chest.)* You have a good heart.

(BRIGHAM *closes his eyes.*)

(ALBERTINE *pops her head in through the door.* ESTHER *sees her.* BRIGHAM *doesn't. O S drums.* ALBERTINE *exits.*)

(BRIGHAM *opens his eyes. He startles.*)

(BRIGHAM *sits up. So does* ESTHER. *She stands up.*)

BRIGHAM: Those drums.

ESTHER: Welcome to Liberia.

BRIGHAM: Did you say something?

ESTHER: About drums?

BRIGHAM: No. Just now.

ESTHER: Like what?

BRIGHAM: I don't know. I just find it strange they start up now.

ESTHER: Every night they start up.

BRIGHAM: But were you saying something?

ESTHER: Yes, I was. I prayed for you. *(She mixes Jeremiah 33:6 and Genesis 9:6.)* God does heal the sick. Behold, I will bring it health and cure, and I will cure them, and will reveal unto them the abundance of peace and truth. Whoso sheddeth man's blood, by man shall his blood be shed. He will find the murderer. *(She touches his chest.)* You strong like Samson.

BRIGHAM: The army stole my hair.

(ALBERTINE *pops her head back in.*)

ESTHER: As long as they don't steal you I'll be fine.

(ESTHER *kisses* BRIGHAM. *She is putting on a show for* ALBERTINE.)

(ESTHER *kisses him.* BRIGHAM *reacts by picking up the Bible and smacking her in the head with it.* ALBERTINE *disappears*—ESTHER *slaps* BRIGHAM *hard.*)

ESTHER: Monster!

BRIGHAM: I'm sick. I'm playing detective. My fiancée was murdered. I'm not looking for love—not right now.

ESTHER: Good, because you'll never find it! *(Composes herself)* You're nothing in America. Even a gray whore in Salt Lake wouldn't touch you.

(BRIGHAM coughs.)

ESTHER: Sick, weak son-of-a-bitch!

(Exit ESTHER. One, two, three. Enter ROSS.)

ROSS: Two women running from your room? Now I know you Brigham Young.

BRIGHAM: She's got enough anger for two hundred women.

ROSS: Rube, I seen 'em run off. Twenty seconds between them. Don't know if I pity or envy you. *(He lights a cigarette.)*

BRIGHAM: Got a light?

ROSS: Get your own, malaria boy. You make three times my pay, officer. And you got almost as many women.

BRIGHAM: It was was just the lovelorn missionary.

ROSS: And her Liberian friend?

BRIGHAM: Dunno what you mean.

ROSS: Club woman. Albertine.

BRIGHAM: Albertine?

(ROSS laughs.)

ROSS: Congratulations. We in the same club.

BRIGHAM: What would she want here?

ROSS: Same thing preacher lady wants. Some of that Utah flesh.

BRIGHAM: Hey now. You introduced me to Esther.

ROSS: As a missionary. I didn't know you'd send her into sexual delirium.

BRIGHAM: You owe me.

ROSS: Tell me you don't like the attention. *(Pause)* She'll take your mind off of more pressing matters.

BRIGHAM: I need my mind on the pressing matters.

ROSS: You stubborn. But that's what's keeping you alive.

BRIGHAM: Everything hurts.

ROSS: She didn't "heal" you none?

(BRIGHAM *just moans in pain.)*

(ROSS *turns the chair and sits on it backwards, so he faces the chair's back and the back faces* BRIGHAM.*)*

ROSS: Can I get ya somethin'?

BRIGHAM: A cigarette?

ROSS: You a medic—

BRIGHAM: Help me.

(ROSS *closer.)*

ROSS: Help you what?

BRIGHAM: Find the killer.

ROSS: That's tough. I could find you a woman from every tribe in this country and one of those Americo-Liberians and a girl from the States and maybe some—

BRIGHAM: The killer.

ROSS: That's a tall order, sir. But orders are orders. *(He flips through the Bible. He looks at the cover of the Bible.)* I see this Bible has come into contact with some makeup.

BRIGHAM: Accidents happen. While I'm down and out, can you follow our suspects?

ROSS: Michaux has his heart set on that heart man.

BRIGHAM: The witch doctor? He's the only genuine man I've met in this confused country. Michaux is too damn harsh.

ROSS: The Natives got it worse here than Colored folk down South.

BRIGHAM: Where do you think these Americo-Liberians came from?

ROSS: Straight off the plantation. That's why they build nice houses. Three stories, some of 'em.

BRIGHAM: You're impressed by a house?

ROSS: Those huts in Shangri-La impress me.

BRIGHAM: You've seen more there than I'll ever see.

ROSS: That's right. You've seen the results.

BRIGHAM: When you've seen a man's nuts swell up the size of honeydew because some gal in Shangri-La bit him.

ROSS: Miss Debbie—

BRIGHAM: You stay away from her. She'll mess you up.

ROSS: The guy with the honey dews, Corporal Williamson? He went back.

BRIGHAM: No wonder everyone hates us. Shake up the jazz joint. She was killed outside the door.

ROSS: Or dropped there.

BRIGHAM: See. You've got it. Why there?

ROSS: Sending a message.

BRIGHAM: To me?

ROSS: Think on it.

BRIGHAM: Do you know something?

ROSS: Nah. Who owns that place anyways?

BRIGHAM: Beats me.

(ROSS *opens the Bible and reads.*)

ROSS: *(Proverbs 21:3)* To do justice and judgment is more acceptable to the Lord than sacrifice.

(The O S drums increase in volume.)

(Lights down:)

Scene 6

(Lights up:)

(The Lone Star. Lights only on PRINCESS.)

(PRINCESS sings "Frankie and Johnny".)

(ALBERTINE occupies a barstool. ROSS next to her.)

PRINCESS: *(Singing)*
Frankie and Johnny were lovers.
O my Gawd how they did love!
They swore to be true to each other,
As true as the stars above.
He was her man but he done her wrong.
Frankie went down to the hock-shop,
Went for a bucket of beer,
Said: "O Mr Bartender
Has my loving Johnny been here?
He is my man but he's doing me wrong."
"I don't want to make you no trouble,
I don't want to tell you no lie,
But I saw Johnny an hour ago
With a girl named Nelly Bly,
He is your man but he's doing you wrong."
Frankie went down to the hotel,
She didn't go there for fun,
'Cause underneath her kimona
She toted a 44 Gun.
He was he man but he done her wrong.

Frankie went down to the hotel.
She rang the front-door bell,
Said: "Stand back all you chippies
Or I'll blow you all to hell.
I want my man for he's doing me wrong."
Frankie looked in through the key-hole
And there before her eye
She saw her Johnny on the sofa
A-loving up Nelly Bly.
He was her man; he was doing her wrong.
Frankie threw back her kimona,
Took out a big 44,
Root-a-toot-toot, three times she shoot
Right through that hardware door.
He was her man but he was doing her wrong.
Johnny grabbed up his Stetson,
Said: "O my Gawd Frankie don't shoot!"
But Frankie pulled hard on the trigger
And the gun went root-a-toot-toot.
She shot her man who was doing her wrong.

(Lights down on PRINCESS:*)*

(Background instrumental)

(Lights up on:)

*(*ALBERTINE *and* ROSS *next to her. Bottle of whiskey in front of him)*

ALBERTINE: I told you, I dunno who own here-o.

ROSS: He dyin' up there with malaria. Could be you.

ALBERTINE: Think you tough?

*(*ROSS *throws back whiskey like it's apple juice.* ALBERTINE *takes the bottle and drinks the whole damn thing.)*

ALBERTINE: Africa eats Yankee boys for fun, Ol' Pa.

ROSS: You sure Africa ain't drinkin' 'em alive? *(He yells to an invisible barman.)* Small boy! One more bottle!

ALBERTINE: Stop, Ross. You know what happen—

ROSS: Don't tell me my business, woman. *(He stands up.)*

ALBERTINE: You can't find the killer when you finish drunk.

ROSS: You make me ask twice. Who owns this dive?

(No answer)

(ROSS kicks the barstool. ALBERTINE stands up.)

(ALBERTINE puts her arm around him. Like a boxer clinching.)

ALBERTINE: Come. We friend. Go outside. The breeze cool you down.

(ROSS pushes ALBERTINE away.)

ALBERTINE: We friend, baby.

ROSS: *(Disgusted)* "Friends." You and half of Monrovia.

ALBERTINE: I love you so much.

ROSS: Tell the truth.

ALBERTINE: If I no tell?

ROSS: Bad things happen to good people.

ALBERTINE: You witched. Your mind makes you think you're the man. But back home you just a sorry—

(Wham! MICHAUX enters like a madman. ALBERTINE folds her arms and pouts. She circles as ROSS and MICHAUX sort things out.)

ROSS: Elliott Ness. I got questions.

MICHAUX: Here in Liberia, the police ask the questions. Do you know how many huts I've burnt? How many goods I've confiscated? How many women I've enjoyed?

ROSS: The answer will always be "One too many".

MICHAUX: *(To* ALBERTINE*)* Where is she?

ALBERTINE: On break. *(Pause)* Sir.

MICHAUX: *(To* ROSS*)* Think you can come here and corrupt my chaste, Christian Americo-Liberian women with your Yankee dollars?

*(*MICHAUX *pulls* ALBERTINE *close.)*

MICHAUX: Our domain. I don't give a goddamn what you do with country girls—or country boys.

ROSS: Who owns this place?

MICHAUX: I'm not at liberty to say.

ROSS: Did you learn your English from a textbook?

MICHAUX: I learned from my parents who learned it from their parents who learned it from—

ROSS: Their master.

MICHAUX: Stop this nonsense. I like you. A lot.

ROSS: Then help me.

MICHAUX: I have no responsibility to you.

ROSS: To human decency. You have a murder and you've done everything except try to solve it.

ALBERTINE: Stop before you go too far.

ROSS: Native this, civilized that. Americo this, American that. You've politicized a simple murder case.

*(*MICHAUX *has* ALBERTINE *in front of him like she's a human shield.)*

ROSS: You didn't politicize it. It's been that way all along.

*(*ROSS *pushes* ALBERTINE *away.)*

MICHAUX: The lightbulb goes off.

*(*MICHAUX *walks behind* ALBERTINE.*)*

ROSS: Bring a woman to a bar fight? Coward.

MICHAUX: I brought this. *(Pulls his sidearm. Revolver)*

ROSS: Don't your soldiers load your ammo? Brig don't think Heart Man did it.

MICHAUX: Who did it?

ROSS: You.

MICHAUX: Me? I am the law of Monrovia. I know who is guilty and who is innocent.

ROSS: Like you know anything. You don't even have an ice box for the body. African Science.

MICHAUX: Do not insult the great Republic of Liberia!

ROSS: I'm not. You're an insult to the Republic of Liberia.

MICHAUX: While your ancestors were in chains, being corrupted by white men, we lived in a state of freedom. We built our own country.

ROSS: Freedom don't mean freedom to hurt everyone else.

MICHAUX: Did I hurt your feelings?

ROSS: Nor freedom to kill.

MICHAUX: Call Eleanor Roosevelt. She'll kiss it better.

ROSS: You gettin' on my nerves, little man.

MICHAUX: Your mother disagrees.

ALBERTINE: *(To both)* Why not just solve the damn thing?

MICHAUX: It can't be solved. Sherlock Holmes here knows this. And he knows why.

ROSS: What the Hell are you talking about? Betty was a good woman. I never even...never even considered her.

MICHAUX: Consider what, Sergeant?

ROSS: Nothing. You're twisting me all up.

MICHAUX: She was too good for you. Educated.
Nice Christian home. What do Americans say?
Cosmopolitan. She wouldn't have anything to do with
a no good boy from a place nobody's ever heard of.
And a sex maniac like you wouldn't let her go—

ROSS: Hell no! *(He takes a swing.)*

MICHAUX: Unlettered peasant! Under arrest.

ROSS: You talk like a serpent. I only believe in action.

MICHAUX: This action?

(MICHAUX grabs ALBERTINE. She squeals.)

ALBERTINE: Michaux, we friend. I don't know nothin'.

MICHAUX: *(To ROSS)* Unlettered. Just like you.

ALBERTINE: Please.

MICHAUX: *(To ROSS)* Leave your gun on base?

(Pause)

ALBERTINE: *(To ROSS)* If you brought your gun, don't
use it.

MICHAUX: I thought Brigham was the soldier without a
gun.

ROSS: Just point me in the right direction.

(MICHAUX points.)

ROSS: What's there?

MICHAUX: America.

ALBERTINE: Ross, he gonna kill me.

ROSS: Let our friend go.

MICHAUX: Our friend?

ALBERTINE: I everybody's friend. You know that.

MICHAUX: Albertine, you are too popular.

ALBERTINE: I'm not.

MICHAUX: Everybody's friend. *(He holds his pistol in* ALBERTINE's *side. He laughs.)* You can do a show.

ALBERTINE: Like Princess?

MICHAUX: No, no, no. Like Albertine and Ross.

ROSS: You're sick.

MICHAUX: The proper word is eccentric.

ALBERTINE: *(To* ROSS*)* It's our only chance.

MICHAUX: Who knows what other crimes you've committed here?

ROSS: Albertine, get over here.

ALBERTINE: I can't.

*(*MICHAUX *pushes* ALBERTINE *to* ROSS.*)*

MICHAUX: Go on Yankee lover boy. Show me how it's done.

ROSS: Go to Hell.

MICHAUX: He's shy now. That's not what the ladies of Shangri-La told me. *(He keeps the gun on* ALBERTINE.*)*

ROSS: Look, cat. We got a murderer.

MICHAUX: And his name is Ross.

ROSS: Never!

MICHAUX: She wouldn't love you.

*(*ROSS *pushes* ALBERTINE *back to* MICHAUX.*)*

ALBERTINE: Hey!

ROSS: Go on. Plug her.

ALBERTINE: Ross!

ROSS: I don't care. *(He sits on the stool.)*

(MICHAUX *aims his at* ALBERTINE, *who screams.* MICHAUX *fires, hitting* ROSS *[his target all along].)*

(ROSS *falls on his back.* ALBERTINE *exits.)*

MICHAUX: The Big Man owns this place, Yankee. *(He points his weapon at* ALBERTINE.*)*

(ALBERTINE *screams.)*

(Lights down on the murder scene:)

(Music louder.)

(Lights up on PRINCESS:*)*

(PRINCESS *finishes "Frankie and Johnny." No sense of irony, of course.)*

PRINCESS: "Roll me over easy,
Roll me over slow,
Roll me over on my right side
Cause my left side hurts me so.
I was her man but I done her wrong."
"Bring out your rubber-tired buggy,
Bring out your rubber-tired hack;
I'll take my Johnny to the graveyard
But I won't bring him back.
He was my man but he done me wrong."
"Lock me in that dungeon,
Lock me in that cell,
Lock me where the north-east wind
Blows from the corner of Hell.
I shot my man 'cause he done me wrong."
It was not murder in the first degree,
It was not murder in the third.
A woman simply shot her man
As a hunter drops a bird.
She shot her man 'cause he done her wrong.
Frankie said to the Sheriff,
"What do you think they'll do?"
The Sheriff said to Frankie,

"It's the electric-chair for you.
You shot your man 'cause he done you wrong."
Frankie sat in the jail-house,
Had no electric fan,
Told her sweet little sister:
"There ain't no good in a man.
I had a man but he done me wrong."
Once more I saw Frankie
She was sitting in the Chair
Waiting for to go and meet her God
With the sweat dripping out of her hair.
He was a man but he done her wrong.
This story has no moral,
This story has no end,
This story only goes to show
That there ain't no good in men.
He was her man but he done her wrong.

(Lights down:)

END OF ACT ONE

ACT TWO

Scene 1

(Lights up)

(Still the jazz club)

(BRIGHAM sits at the bar out of his uniform. Casual 1940s clothing. He takes out a small rectangular piece of paper. He looks at it.)

(BRIGHAM imitates the voice of F D R.)

BRIGHAM: *(As F D R)* August 6, 1943. Lieutenant Thurman. I've heard of the recent murder of your sergeant as well as a nurse. I pray you will, with due diligence and cooperation from the Liberian authorities find the killer of both service members. I am entrusting the job to you. *(He coughs. Normal)* Who am I kidding? *(F D R voice.)*

F D R: *(OS)* Be a credit to your race.

BRIGHAM: Shut the Hell up, Mister President.

(Enter ALBERTINE behind BRIGHAM, with a drink. She wears a blouse and skirt.)

(She wraps her arms around him. She puts her drink on the table.)

ALBERTINE: Don't mind ya.

BRIGHAM: I sent him to the Lone Star club.

ALBERTINE: May I sit here?

BRIGHAM: Sit wherever you damn well please. Your country.

ALBERTINE: Don't think like that.

BRIGHAM: Don't think honestly?

ALBERTINE: We have our way.

BRIGHAM: Law of the jungle, huh?

ALBERTINE: Not true.

BRIGHAM: Corruption. Greed. Licentiousness. Murder.

ALBERTINE: It must be America in Africa.

(BRIGHAM *stands.*)

ALBERTINE: What are you going to do? *(She sees F D R's telegram on the bar. She picks it up. Looks at it)* What's it say?

BRIGHAM: His family. What do I tell them?

(ALBERTINE *stands up and circles around* BRIGHAM *as they talk.*)

ALBERTINE: Tell them the best man in the army will find his killer.

BRIGHAM: We know who did it. You saw him.

ALBERTINE: He was like a rabid dog.

BRIGHAM: Help me.

ALBERTINE: You want me to be hurt?

BRIGHAM: Never mind.

(ALBERTINE *looks around, then lifts the side of her blouse, exposing some flesh.*)

(BRIGHAM *looks away.*)

ALBERTINE: When was the last time a woman hurt you? Look at me! Look at what he done.

(BRIGHAM *looks. A massive bruise*)

BRIGHAM: Nice bruise.

(ALBERTINE *puts her blouse down.*)

ALBERTINE: Your sergeant hurt women.

(BRIGHAM *takes a drink.*)

BRIGHAM: Michaux did that.

ALBERTINE: He did not.

BRIGHAM: Then you did it yourself. This ain't some damn game. People are dying.

ALBERTINE: Ain't no Liberian died.

(BRIGHAM *grabs* ALBERTINE's *wrist.*)

BRIGHAM: You have a point.

(ALBERTINE *pulls her hand back.*)

ALBERTINE: That's not all I've got. I always admired a strong man.

BRIGHAM: The victims were American. We know Michaux killed Ross.

(ALBERTINE *climbs up on the table/bar. Leaves shoes on the floor. Faces* BRIGHAM)

BRIGHAM: I've got to—

(BRIGHAM *starts to stand.* ALBERTINE *pushes him back onto the chair with her foot.*)

ALBERTINE: Know why he beat me?

BRIGHAM: You beat yourself. Some attention thing. Ross warned me about you.

ALBERTINE: Because of you. He was jealous. You and I friend. Ya know?

BRIGHAM: Find some other sad sack G I.

ALBERTINE: Now he gone. I need a strong man.

BRIGHAM: It ain't me.

ALBERTINE: Don't throw me away.

BRIGHAM: Throw you away? You're not even mine to throw away.

ALBERTINE: But you single now.

BRIGHAM: With good reason.

ALBERTINE: If you don't get me, Michaux will.

BRIGHAM: You do have free agency in this.

ALBERTINE: Liberian men take what they want. (*She moves in. Her legs on either side of* BRIGHAM *now.*)

ALBERTINE: What's that missionary got?

BRIGHAM: What do you mean?

ALBERTINE: Esther. (*She shows her leg.*) Smooth like an American's.

BRIGHAM: Did Ross beat any native Liberians? Any country people?

(ALBERTINE *gets off the table. She stands.* BRIGHAM *stands and faces her.*)

ALBERTINE: If you hate me, just tell me.

BRIGHAM: I don't hate you.

ALBERTINE: What do you call it?

BRIGHAM: I need to find Betty's killer and deal with Michaux.

ALBERTINE: They may be one and the same.

BRIGHAM: You think I don't know that?

(ALBERTINE *lights up a cigarette.*)

ALBERTINE: Your woman is dead. The sergeant is dead. (*Pause*) Go back to the white man's country. Waste their time. (*She walks away.*)

BRIGHAM: Hey!

(BRIGHAM *chases* ALBERTINE. *Grabs her*)

ALBERTINE: Now you want me.

BRIGHAM: I trust you.

ALBERTINE: Why?

BRIGHAM: You're the only person here besides Ross who hasn't lied to me. I believe you about Ross. He had his demons.

ALBERTINE: You don't belong here. Go home.

BRIGHAM: Justice is here. My sergeant died here. My fiancee died here.

ALBERTINE: There's no sergeant and no fiancee. Do you think there will be justice?

BRIGHAM: Only tomorrow knows.

(PRINCESS *enters, sees* BRIGHAM *and runs back outside.*)

(BRIGHAM *follows, leaving* ALBERTINE *alone.*)

BRIGHAM: Princess!

(Lights down)

(Lights up:)

Scene 2

(A Monrovia alleyway)

(Enter PRINCESS *running like the wind, followed by* BRIGHAM.*)*

PRINCESS: No!

*(*BRIGHAM *grabs* PRINCESS *by the wrist and she falls to the floor/ground/street. She screams. Heavy, heavy Liberian accent.)*

PRINCESS: Mister Yank! You don't know what trouble you in. You don't know.

BRIGHAM: What trouble?

PRINCESS: I don' wanna die!

BRIGHAM: You're not going to die. I can help you.

PRINCESS: I don't need no help. They cut your inside with a razor.

BRIGHAM: How'd you know it was a razor? Was it you?

PRINCESS: You think she was the first juju murder in Liberia-o?

BRIGHAM: Why?

PRINCESS: Was she a virgin?

(No answer)

PRINCESS: Reason enough. Coloh boy. *(She just lies on the ground, legs spread apart.)*

BRIGHAM: Who did it?

PRINCESS: I can' tell.

(BRIGHAM *grabs* PRINCESS *again.*)

PRINCESS: I dunno, Yankee!

BRIGHAM: Why'd you run away from me? I don't even know you.

(PRINCESS *screams.* MICHAUX *enters U S L behind* BRIGHAM. *Pistol drawn)*

BRIGHAM: Murderer!

(Whack! MICHAUX *pistol-whips* BRIGHAM.*)*

MICHAUX: *(To* PRINCESS*)* Go!

(PRINCESS *exits.)*

MICHAUX: *(To* BRIGHAM*)* I found the killer.

BRIGHAM: You saw your own reflection?

MICHAUX: Your sergeant? Accidents happen in Monrovia.

BRIGHAM: Murderer!

MICHAUX: Suicide. I saw it. A suicide witnessed by an of the Liberian Frontier Force is an official suicide.

BRIGHAM: You no-account Congo!

MICHAUX: I found the killer. *(He still has his gun trained on* BRIGHAM.*)* A colored boy from America.

BRIGHAM: Hey, man. You not only killed Ross. You killed my fiancée.

*(*MICHAUX *kicks* BRIGHAM.*)*

MICHAUX: Rapist! Murderer! *(He puts the gun next to* BRIGHAM'*s head.)* Want to suicide?

(Lights down:)

(A "click". MICHAUX *pulled the trigger to an empty weapon. He laughs manically.)*

(Lights up:)

Scene 3

(The same police cell that HEART MAN *was tortured in. Two chairs)*

*(*BRIGHAM'*s turn. In chair. He coughs. Sick and hurt.* MICHAUX *stands, holds his riding crop.)*

MICHAUX: Why did you cut them?

BRIGHAM: Them?

MICHAUX: So you admit to one?

BRIGHAM: Just kill me.

MICHAUX: Confess.

BRIGHAM: You couldn't read it if I did write it.

MICHAUX: Your end may come sooner than expected.

BRIGHAM: I just want Betty's killer.

MICHAUX: We all want things, Brigham. (*He pulls up a chair.*) I know why you're here, Mister Thurman.

(BRIGHAM *coughs. Falls off chair*)

MICHAUX: You can't stand how the white man treats you back in Georgia—

BRIGHAM: Utah.

MICHAUX: Never heard of it. They treat you poor. Hell, they don't even let you be a soldier in your own country.

(BRIGHAM *collapses.*)

MICHAUX: So you become the man here. Your reign has ended Mister Thurman. You will hang. The sooner the better. Americans. We are a small country. Why us?

(BRIGHAM *too feeble to do much but speak.*)

BRIGHAM: Your ancestors are American. Maybe that's why you abuse the real Liberians.

MICHAUX: You abuse us.

BRIGHAM: You're the true slave to racism.

(BRIGHAM'*s final collapse. He laughs and laughs.* MICHAUX *kicks him.* MICHAUX *pulls a knife.*)

MICHAUX: I kill you.

(*O S knock knock.* MICHAUX *interrupted*)

MICHAUX: Go!

(*O S knock knock*)

MICHAUX: I am busy you fool! Go! Now! I beat you!

(*A groan from* BRIGHAM)

(*Enter Liberian* PRESIDENT EDWIN BARCLAY. MICHAUX *salutes with left hand.*)

MICHAUX: Mister President.

PRESIDENT BARCLAY: Right hand.

(MICHAUX *switches hands.*)

PRESIDENT BARCLAY: Help him.

MICHAUX: Mister President. He's the killer!

PRESIDENT BARCLAY: He will find the killer.

(MICHAUX *hurriedly helps* BRIGHAM *to his feet. He brushes him off like he's a piece of furniture. Fixes his clothes.* MICHAUX *all smiles.*)

MICHAUX: He's okay, Mister President.

PRESIDENT BARCLAY: (*To* BRIGHAM) Have a seat.

BRIGHAM: You're first Liberian I met who knocks before entering.

PRESIDENT BARCLAY: What?

MICHAUX: A little joke. Americans are famous for their sense of humor. He can have my seat!

(MICHAUX *gingerly puts* BRIGHAM *in the chair.*)

PRESIDENT BARCLAY: (*To* MICHAUX) You are lucky I found you and not the American general.

MICHAUX: Thank you, sir.

PRESIDENT BARCLAY: We Liberians keep our problems in-house, understand?

MICHAUX: Yes, sir.

PRESIDENT BARCLAY: We shall speak later.

MICHAUX: Sir?

PRESIDENT BARCLAY: Dismissed.

MICHAUX: Yes, sir! (*He exits.*)

(PRESIDENT BARCLAY *stoops to talk to* BRIGHAM.)

PRESIDENT BARCLAY: How are you?

BRIGHAM: Seen better days.

PRESIDENT BARCLAY: We thank you for protecting our country from the fascist menace. I've been to America.

(BRIGHAM *coughs.*)

PRESIDENT BARCLAY: I've been to Washington. Met your president. Nice guy. He loves Liberia—almost as much as I do. I love your president. And Eleanor. She really is a beacon for the common man. If you need anything—anything at all, tell people you know The Big Man. Barclay.

(BRIGHAM *falls off the chair.*)

PRESIDENT BARCLAY: You need a doctor. I shall summon one. Immediately.

(BRIGHAM's *breathing audible*)

PRESIDENT BARCLAY: Maybe a nurse—to cure your Liberian Fever? *(Laughs)*

BRIGHAM: Why help me?

PRESIDENT BARCLAY: I love America. America built this country. America sent her own people back to Africa to found the greatest African country that has ever existed.

(BRIGHAM *in pain on the floor.*)

BRIGHAM: They cut off your money.

(PRESIDENT BARCLAY *pulls a handkerchief out of his pocket. The Liberian flag*)

PRESIDENT BARCLAY: I know you have Texas with its Lone Star. We have our own lone star. *(Shows the handkerchief to* BRIGHAM.) Too bad your ancestors didn't make the correct choice and come to Africa. You could be doing the kicking instead of being kicked.*(He stands. He sings an a cappella song,* The Lone Star Forever *which he actually wrote. It is a patriotic Liberian song that sounds very much like a hymn.)*
When Freedom raised her glowing form

On Montserrado's verdant height,
She set within the dome of night,
Midst lowering skies and thunder-storm,
The star of Liberty!
And seizing from the waking morn,
Its burnished shield of golden flame,
She lifted it in her proud name,
And roused a nation long forlorn,
To nobler destiny!
The lone star forever!
The lone star forever!
Unfurled in the currents of heaven's pure breeze,
O long may it float o'er land and o'er seas
Desert it? No! Never!
Uphold it? ay, ever!
O shout for the lone-starred banner, Hurrah!
(*Pause*) I wrote that song.

(PRESIDENT BARCLAY *looks at* BRIGHAM, *who is passed out.*)

(*Lights down:*)

(*Lights up:*)

Scene 4

(BRIGHAM. *In bed. Stool next to the bed.* ALBERTINE *with him.*)

BRIGHAM: Barclay himself. This is big.

(ALBERTINE *stands up. She laughs.*)

ALBERTINE: He think he big. Barclay's a quiet little man. Did you ever think why he wants to free an American Negro soldier?

BRIGHAM: Get F D R off his case.

ALBERTINE: And I thought Liberians were dumb. The president just doesn't walk in during an interrogation and send the suspect to R & R.

(BRIGHAM *sits on the edge of the bed.*)

BRIGHAM: Why then?

ALBERTINE: To kill you.

BRIGHAM: In a hospital?

ALBERTINE: Plenty of folks die in the hospital. Why not you? *(She sits next to him.)* You've had soldiers go A-WOL right?

BRIGHAM: Right.

ALBERTINE: And never come back, right?

(BRIGHAM *stands up. Wobbles)*

BRIGHAM: Right.

(ALBERTINE *also stands and puts her arms around* BRIGHAM.)

ALBERTINE: Going somewhere?

BRIGHAM: If I can.

(ALBERTINE *pulls him back and pushes him onto the bed.*)

ALBERTINE: Stay. Albertine will take good care of you. *(She pulls out a knife.)* This is isn't for you, dear. It's for the rest of the world.

BRIGHAM: Thanks?

ALBERTINE: Nobody will hurt you. *(She puts her arm around him.)* She kisses him.

ALBERTINE: I love you, so I'll help you.

BRIGHAM: What type of help?

ALBERTINE: The woman who cut up your fiancee.

BRIGHAM: A woman did it?

ALBERTINE: Dark women like cutting.

(BRIGHAM *sits up.*)

BRIGHAM: What do you mean, cutting?

ALBERTINE: Don't you know about the aborigines?

BRIGHAM: They seem a lot nicer than the Mericos I met.

ALBERTINE: Their women feel nothing.

BRIGHAM: Female circumcision.

ALBERTINE: Mutilation. As a medical officer you should—

BRIGHAM: I know that.

ALBERTINE: You don't know how many more men they can accommodate in a day because of their loss of feeling.

BRIGHAM: As a medical man for American soldiers and their whores, I know all too well.

ALBERTINE: I'm a civilized Christian woman. No aborigine in me. I feel everything.

BRIGHAM: So who has been cut?

ALBERTINE: Why do you think Princess ran from you that night? She can't feel. (*Pause*) She's aborigine.

BRIGHAM: I figured she knew I had a mark on me.

ALBERTINE: Oh, you cursed alright.

(BRIGHAM *takes away* ALBERTINE's *knife gently. Enter* ESTHER. BRIGHAM *grabs the knife.*)

ESTHER: Brig, how are you?

BRIGHAM: Sick.

ESTHER: They mussed you up but bad. An intelligent man would've learned by now.

ALBERTINE: Excuse me?

ESTHER: Did you say something?

ALBERTINE: Yeah, and I'm gonna say more—hussy.

BRIGHAM: Albertine.

ALBERTINE: *(To* BRIGHAM*)* Shut up while I kill this Yankee no-good—

ESTHER: Do not judge!

ALBERTINE: You can hide behind your Christian skin all you want. But you and I know deep down what you are. You're no better than me—a hussy!

ESTHER: Watapolee!

ALBERTINE: Now you talk Liberian.

(ESTHER *slaps* ALBERTINE. BRIGHAM *pushes them apart.)*

BRIGHAM: What ails you? They're thousands of American soldiers you could be fighting over. I'm sick. I'm sad. I'm desperate.

ESTHER: I feel for you.

ALBERTINE: Not the only thing she feel.

BRIGHAM: *(To* ALBERTINE*)* You're not helping.

ALBERTINE: I'm helping you. Can't you see that?

BRIGHAM: No. I can't. Starting a fight like this. Bringing a knife. None of this helps me. I've got to find the killer.

ESTHER: That again!

ALBERTINE: Give it a rest.

BRIGHAM: A rest?

ESTHER: She's dead.

ALBERTINE: Like the hussy say, she dead.

BRIGHAM: No. There's more going on than what you're telling me.

ALBERTINE: You right.

BRIGHAM: I am?

ALBERTINE: You don't need my help. Good luck, Brigham. (*She exits.*)

BRIGHAM: (*To* ESTHER) You?

ESTHER: I couldn't stay away.

BRIGHAM: Are there no other men in Monrovia?

ESTHER: Not like you, Wesley.

BRIGHAM: Look, I don't know who killed my fiancée—

ESTHER: You still think about her.

BRIGHAM: Wouldn't you?

ESTHER: She's dead. But, baby, I'm full of life.

BRIGHAM: Let's keep it that way. Why do you think the president freed me from Michaux?

ESTHER: He's going to kill you. He'll have it done. If you was killed in jail, that looks bad, but if you was killed after you found the killer, you die a hero. Who knows? Maybe they'll award you the Order of African Redemption.

BRIGHAM: I've got enough fruit salad.

ESTHER: We need to get you out.

(ESTHER *pulls* BRIGHAM *out of bed. They exit.*)

(*Lights down:*)

Scene 5

(*Lights up:*)

(*Back to* ESTHER'*s ritzy house. American religious imperialism on display.*)

(*Both* ESTHER *and* BRIGHAM *recline in chairs to the sides. She has a drink in her left hand.*)

(In the center, D S C, stands PRINCESS. *She sings, as always. This version is* Delia *or* Delia's Gone.*)*

PRINCESS: Delia was a gambler, gambled all around.
She was a gambling girl, she laid her money down.
She's all I got, is gone
Delia's dear mother, took a trip out west.
When she returned, little Delia had gone to rest.
She's all I got, is gone
Delia's mother weep, Delia's father moaned.
Wouldn'ta hate it so bad if that child had died at home.
She's all I got, is gone
Delia, Delia, how can it be?
Say you loved them rounders, and don't love me.
She's all I got, is gone
Curtis, he's in the bar room, bringing out the silver
    cup.
Delia she's in the graveyard, may not never wake up.
She's all I got, is gone
Rubber tire buggy, double seated hack:
Taken Delia to the cemetery but failed to bring her
    back.
She's all I got, is gone
Delia, Delia, poor girl she's gone.
All I hate, she has left me all alone.
She's all I got, is gone
Judge says to Curtis, "What's that fuss about?"
"On account of those gamblers, trying to drive me
    out."
She's all I got, is gone
Curtis says to judge, "What may be my fine?"
"I just told you, poor boy, you got 99."
She's all I got, is gone
Up on the housetop, higher than I could see.
Looking at those rounders, looking out for me.
She's all I got, is gone
Curtis looking high, Curtis looking low.

Shot poor Delia down, with that hating .44.
She's all I got, is gone.

(ESTHER *and* BRIGHAM *clap.*)

ESTHER: I just love me a murder ballad! I invited her.
Just for you. *(Pause)* The cold unfeeling delivery makes
it seem as if Princess herself could be behind this girl
Delia's death.

(ESTHER *hands* PRINCESS *a dollar.*)

PRINCESS: My baby can eat!

BRIGHAM: Princess.

(PRINCESS *exits.*)

ESTHER: She sang on the condition you not speak to
her.

BRIGHAM: But I spoke to her.

ESTHER: And she didn't speak back.

(ESTHER *stands. She walks over to* BRIGHAM *and climbs on
top of him.*)

BRIGHAM: Not here.

ESTHER: Yes, here. *(She kisses him.)* Here. Now. *(She
starts rubbing her body on him.)* Come on, come on.

BRIGHAM: Esther—

(Enter MICHAUX, *carrying* ALBERTINE. *He throws*
ALBERTINE *to the floor.* ESTHER *goes to* ALBERTINE.*)*

ESTHER: *(To* MICHAUX*)* Get out of my house!

MICHAUX: *(To* BRIGHAM*)* Here are your murderers!

ESTHER: Murderers?

(MICHAUX *points at* ESTHER.)

MICHAUX: Killer one. *(Points at* ALBERTINE*)* Killer two.

ESTHER: I didn't kill nothin'

ALBERTINE: You are insane!

MICHAUX: *(To* ALBERTINE *and* ESTHER) Degenerates.

(ESTHER *tries to attack* MICHAUX. BRIGHAM *holds her back.)*

ESTHER: I'll kill you!

MICHAUX: Not only is she a pervert, she's a murderer! And that wench, too.

ALBERTINE: Excuse you? You wanna die?

(ALBERTINE *also tries to attack* MICHAUX. BRIGHAM *holds her back, too. He has both women.)*

BRIGHAM: Wait. Albertine and Esther both want to kill you?

MICHAUX: They are together in this.

(BRIGHAM *lets them go.)*

BRIGHAM: *(To* ESTHER *and* ALBERTINE) That's why you took turns watching while I was with the other. I certainly flattered myself. *(He looks at both.)* The whore and the madonna. African and American.

MICHAUX: They prefer the company of women to the company of men.

BRIGHAM: Did you kill Betty because she wouldn't play?

ALBERTINE: Don't even believe him.

BRIGHAM: Bull daggers.

MICHAUX: Not all Americo-Liberians are degenerate.

BRIGHAM: You shut up.

MICHAUX: But you believe me?

BRIGHAM: *(To* MICHAUX) Missionary and good-time girl.

MICHAUX: What shall we do to them?

BRIGHAM: Got your gun?

(MICHAUX *pulls out his revolver and spins the cylinder. He fans his pistol, showing off and fires a round.*)

BRIGHAM: Jesus! Wild Bill!

MICHAUX: No Jesus in this room.

BRIGHAM: You know what, Michaux?

MICHAUX: What, Yankee?

BRIGHAM: These women…they don't know what women are for.

MICHAUX: Say, Brother Brigham. You're right. We could teach them.

(BRIGHAM *pushes* ESTHER *to* MICHAUX.)

ESTHER: No!

MICHAUX: Oh, yes. I like this.

(MICHAUX *holds* ESTHER *close with his pistol in her side.*)

(ALBERTINE *runs to him.*)

ALBERTINE: Don't hurt her.

(MICHAUX *punches* ALBERTINE *in the face.*)

(MICHAUX *points his gun at* ALBERTINE.)

MICHAUX: Admit it.

ALBERTINE: I confess.

MICHAUX: Why'd you cut her up?

(ESTHER *makes a play for the gun. She grabs it. Points it at* MICHAUX.)

ESTHER: The only thing I murdered was— *(Pause)* —my heart.

(ESTHER *points the gun to her chest.* BRIGHAM *grabs the pistol. Pop! Misses* ESTHER)

(*She collapses in shock.*)

ALBERTINE: No!

(ALBERTINE *attends to* ESTHER.)

ALBERTINE: Animals!

MICHAUX: *(To* BRIGHAM*)* Let's have our fun.

BRIGHAM: Why did they kill my fiancée?

MICHAUX: Sex?

BRIGHAM: And the mutilation?

MICHAUX: To frame an innocent medicine man. They are evil.

BRIGHAM: You sure, Captain?

MICHAUX: It could be jealousy. Such a personal attack. You performed the autopsy.

BRIGHAM: Jealousy?

MICHAUX: Jealous of you. Of your strapping American youth and vigor.

BRIGHAM: If they were jealous of me, why didn't they kill me? They kill her, all they've got is me. You're right, Michaux. I did perform that autopsy.

MICHAUX: See? Let's take care of them!

(MICHAUX *grabs* ESTHER.)

BRIGHAM: Betty was with child.

(MICHAUX *tries to shake* BRIGHAM's *hand.* MICHAUX *walks back.)*

MICHAUX: I don't have a cigar. That's American, right? The cigar?

BRIGHAM: Not *my* child, Michaux.

MICHAUX: What do you mean?

BRIGHAM: You've been pointing me in circles ever since her death. The only reason you pretend to play straight is because of Barclay.

MICHAUX: We're friends, now. The killers are right here.

BRIGHAM: One is. And now his reason is as clear as day.

MICHAUX: What can I say? I rode her—just like the cavalry. Just like every whore in Monrovia.

ALBERTINE: You didn't!

MICHAUX: I still love you.

(ALBERTINE *grabs* ESTHER's *gun and fires at* MICHAUX. MICHAUX *grabs* ALBERTINE's *gun and shoots her. They both collapse.*)

ESTHER: You okay?

(BRIGHAM *picks up the gun.*)

BRIGHAM: No.

(ESTHER *runs to* MICHAUX' *body. She pulls a ceremonial knife from his body. Throws it on the stage. Kicks his body)*

(ESTHER *runs to* ALBERTINE—*pulls a ceremonial knife from inside her dress. Throws the knife onto the stage.*)

ESTHER: There! Those are your murderers. Americo-Liberians feigning savagery. Blaming the aborigines when they are the true savages.

(BRIGHAM *picks up a knife.*)

BRIGHAM: I could see this doing the devil's work.

(Lights down:)

Scene 6

(Lights up:)

(The same house. Later. No bodies. Only ESTHER *and* BRIGHAM.*)*

BRIGHAM: Who is civilized? Who is savage?

(ESTHER *drapes her arms around* BRIGHAM.)

ESTHER: You smell good.

(BRIGHAM *kisses her arm.*)

ESTHER: Hold your horses. I'm a God-fearing Christian girl. Remember?

BRIGHAM: If this violence hadn't gone down, we'd never met.

ESTHER: Isn't it funny? I have something personal to ask.

BRIGHAM: Shoot.

ESTHER: How'd you feel when you learned Betty was expecting?

(BRIGHAM *laughs.*)

BRIGHAM: I ain't that stupid. (*Laughs*) She wasn't pregnant.

ESTHER: Good, right?

BRIGHAM: Good and dead.

(ESTHER *embraces* BRIGHAM.)

ESTHER: You'll always have me. (*She grabs his butt.*) What's that?

(BRIGHAM *pulls one of the knives out of his back pocket. Smiles*)

BRIGHAM: They let me keep the evidence.

ESTHER: Don't scare me, baby.

BRIGHAM: Just a second ago our love was eternal.

ESTHER: I don't wanna see it!

BRIGHAM: Why not? It's got your blood all over it!

ESTHER: You killed her!

BRIGHAM: I loved her! I don't kill women I love.

ESTHER: You did.

BRIGHAM: You're insane.

ESTHER: Yes, you did. Because you loved me!

BRIGHAM: I didn't even know you!

(ESTHER *takes out a ceremonial knife from her own pocket.*)

BRIGHAM: I can't get anything past you, can I?

ESTHER: You're so stupid, Wesley.

BRIGHAM: I knew those knives you found were plants.

(ESTHER *and* BRIGHAM *circle one another.*)

ESTHER: What do you know about knives? You're a medic. You save lives, not take them.

BRIGHAM: Times change. I've changed. Before I met you, I couldn't even kill time.

ESTHER: Why won't you love me? Why? (*Psalm 25:16*) Turn thee unto me, and have mercy upon me; for I am desolate and afflicted. (*She holds the knife to her chest. She hesitates. Hands shaking*)

(BRIGHAM *approaches* ESTHER.)

BRIGHAM: Esther—

(ESTHER *points the knife at* BRIGHAM *with both hands.*)

ESTHER: Take it.

(BRIGHAM *moves his hand near* ESTHER.)

(ESTHER *pulls the knife back sharply, clipping* BRIGHAM'*s hand.*)

BRIGHAM: Ow!

(ESTHER *laughs.*)

ESTHER: She bled, too. Like a stuck pig. She was weak. I'm strong! I ate that weak heart of hers.

(ESTHER *stabs* BRIGHAM. *He grabs her knife. He stabs her with both knives. An explosion of blood*)

(As ESTHER *collapses—)*

ESTHER: I loved you.

(ESTHER *dead.* BRIGHAM *surveys the carnage.)*

(Lights down)

END OF PLAY

www.ingramcontent.com/pod-product-compliance
Lightning Source LLC
Chambersburg PA
CBHW052216090426
42741CB00010B/2570